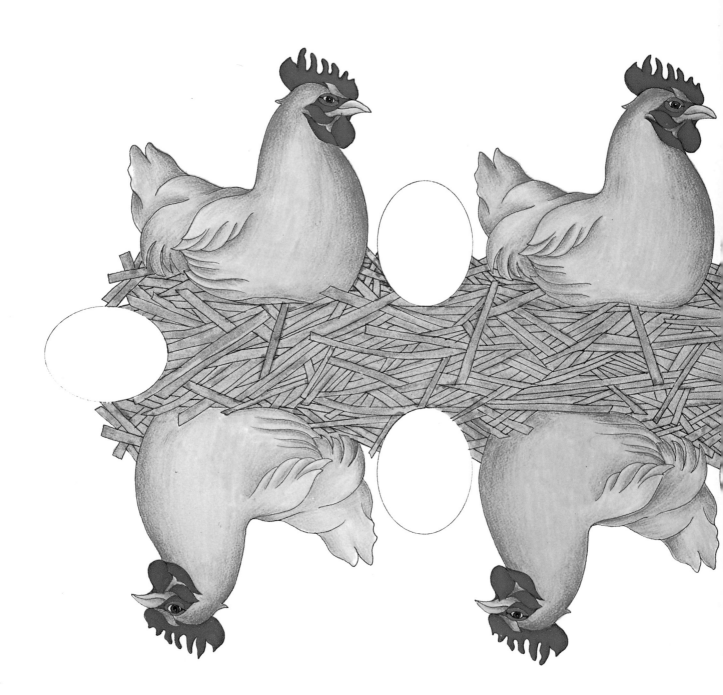

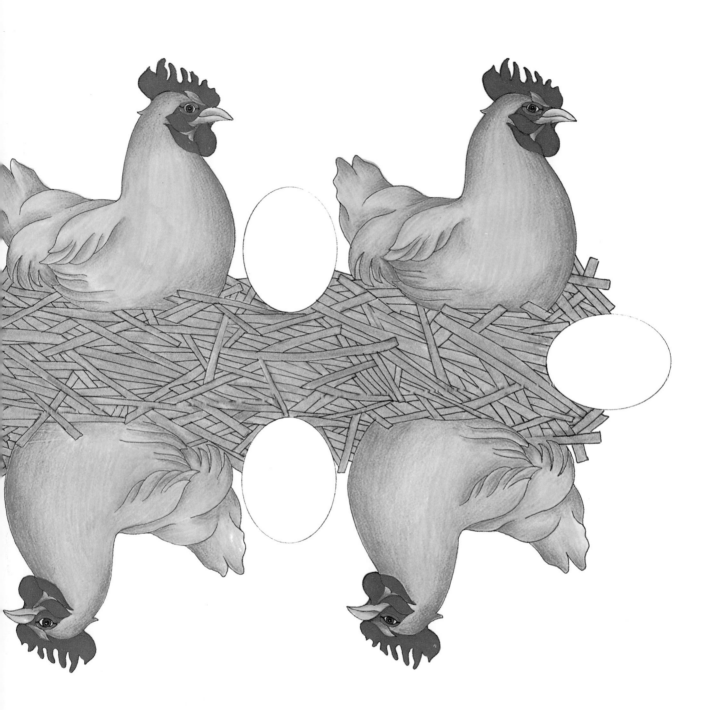

My special thanks to
Margaret G. Bradbury, Ph.D.
Professor of Biology
San Francisco State University

Copyright © 1981 by The Ruth Heller Trust.
All rights reserved. This book, or parts thereof, may not be reproduced in any form
without permission in writing from the publisher. A PaperStar Book, published in 1999
by Penguin Putnam Books for Young Readers, 345 Hudson Street, New York, NY 10014.
PaperStar is a registered trademark of The Putnam Berkley Group, Inc.
The PaperStar logo is a trademark of The Putnam Berkley Group, Inc.
Originally published in 1981 by Grosset & Dunlap.
Published simultaneously in Canada. Printed in Hong Kong.
Library of Congress Catalog Card Number: 80-85257
ISBN 0-698-11778-6
7 9 10 8

RUTH HELLER

WORLD OF NATURE

CHICKENS AREN'T
THE ONLY ONES

Written and illustrated by

RUTH HELLER

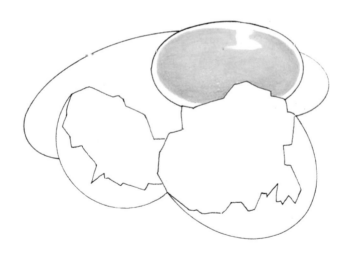

Penguin Putnam Books for Young Readers

CHICKENS
lay the
eggs you
buy,

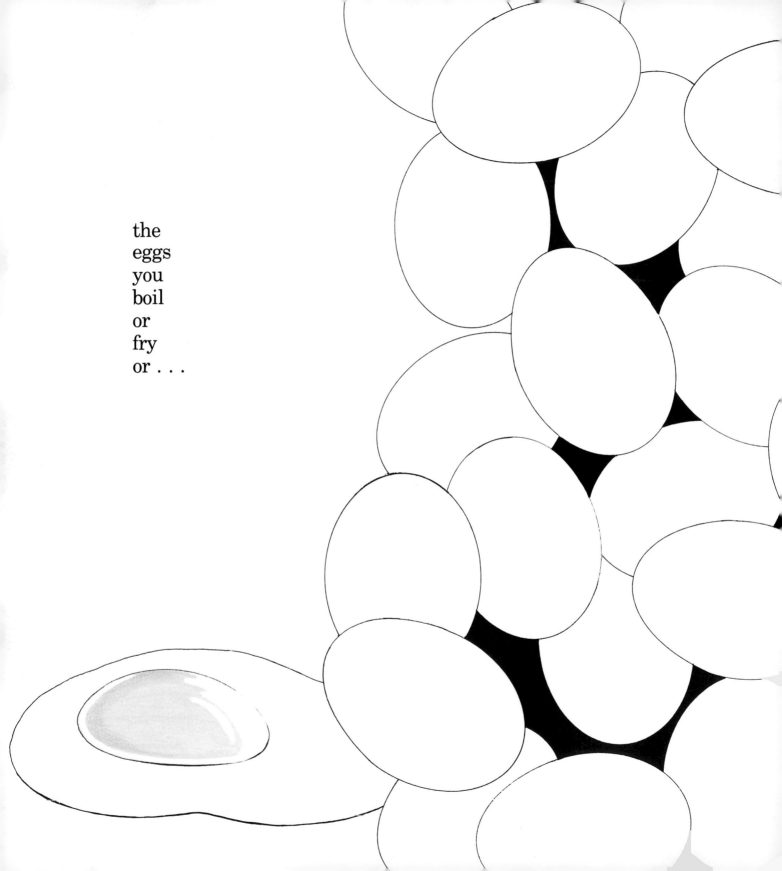

the
eggs
you
boil
or
fry
or . . .

dye!

or leave
alone so
you can
see
what grew
inside
naturally.

CHICKENS
aren't the
only ones.

Every
BIRD
wild
or . . .

tame
does the same.

The
OSTRICH
lays

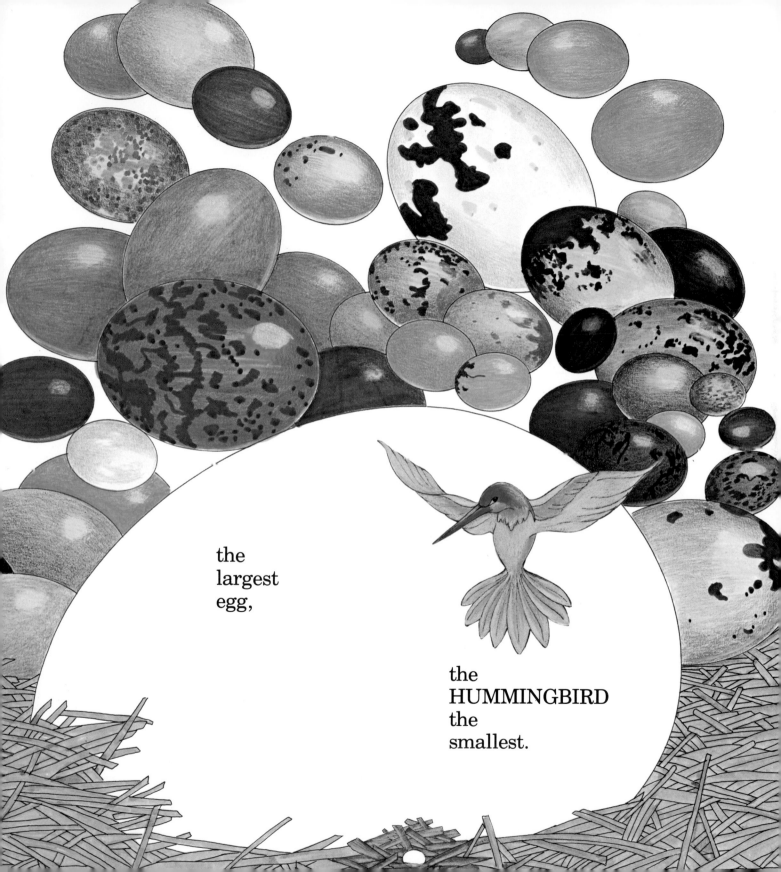

the
largest
egg,

the
HUMMINGBIRD
the
smallest.

CHICKENS aren't the only ones.

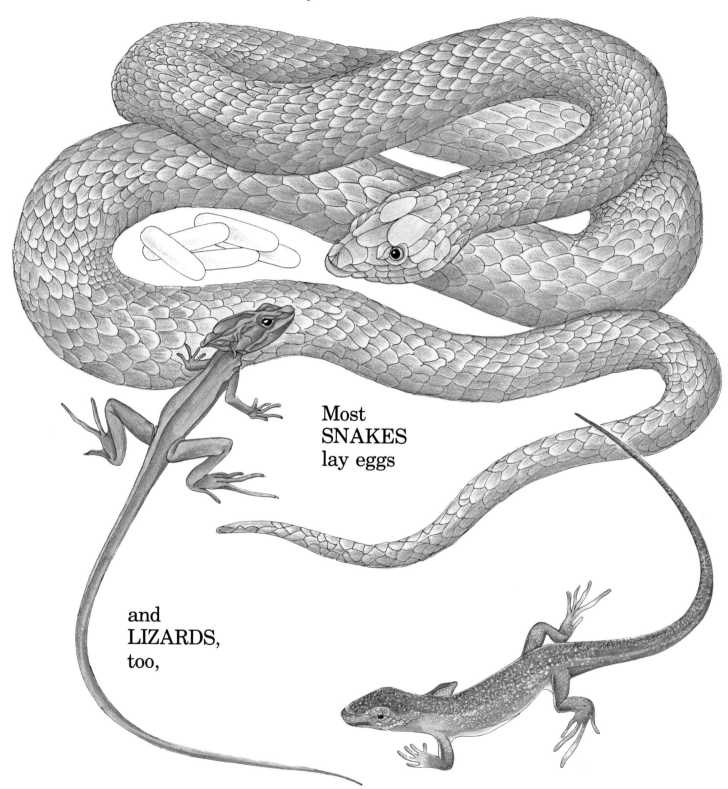

Most
SNAKES
lay eggs

and
LIZARDS,
too,

and
CROCODILES

and
TURTLES do,

and DINOSAURS
who are extinct, but they were reptiles, too.

FROGS and TOADS and SALAMANDERS

lay eggs,

and when they hatch
they're tadpoles
who grow legs
and climb a lily pad—
just like their
    mom
    and
    dad.

They don't have
claws or
scaly skins.
They are called
AMPHIBIANS.

FISH
eggs
float
up
to
the
surface
or . . .
sink
to
the
bottom
of
the
ocean
floor.

This mother
SEAHORSE
lays her eggs
into the
father's pouch.
He keeps
them there
until they
hatch, and
then he's
through.

I think
that's
nice
of him,
don't you?

These fathers, too,
are helping out
by guarding eggs
protected by
that foamy mass
that's
floating
by.

And
they won't
leave

until
they're
sure
that
all the
eggs
have hatched.

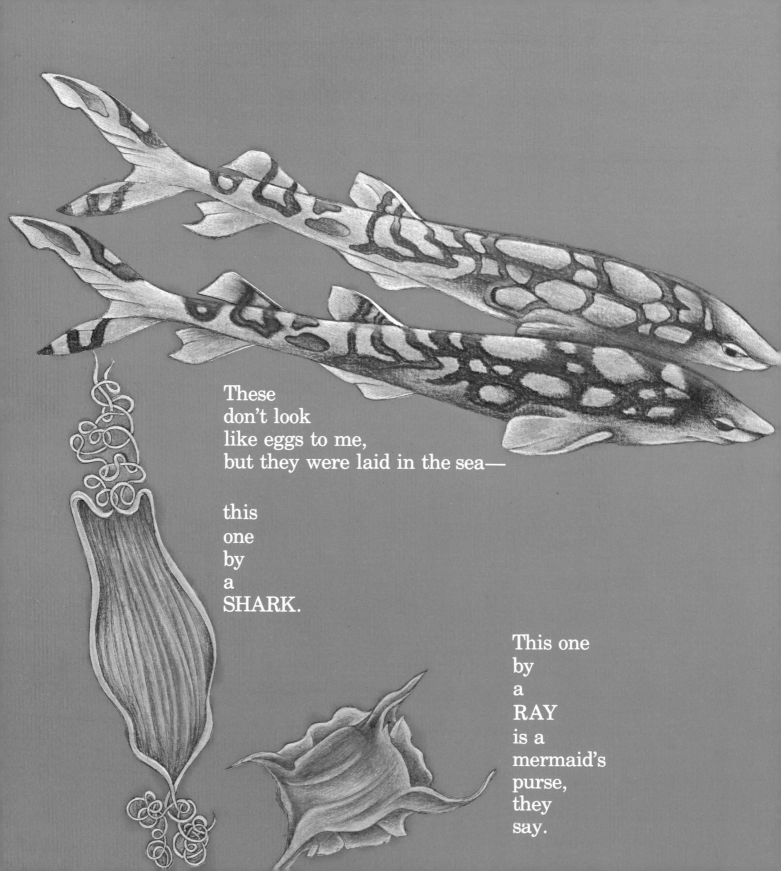

These
don't look
like eggs to me,
but they were laid in the sea—

this
one
by
a
SHARK.

This one
by
a
RAY
is a
mermaid's
purse,
they
say.

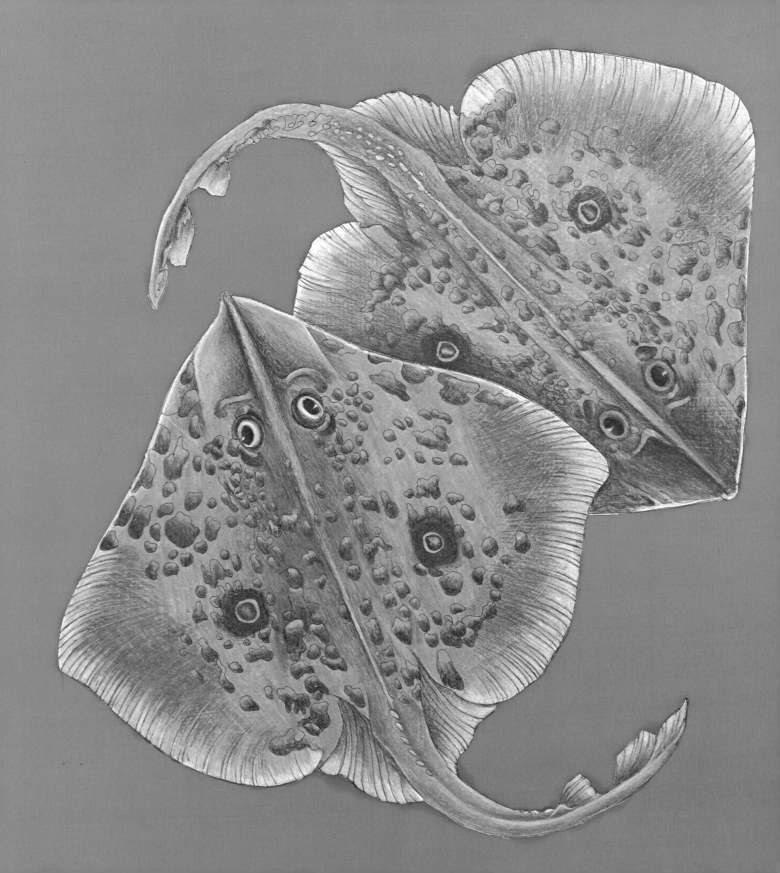

The
OCTOPUS
is said
to shed
one
hundred
thousand
eggs
and then
to hang
them up
in
strings
attached
to
rocks
or
caves.

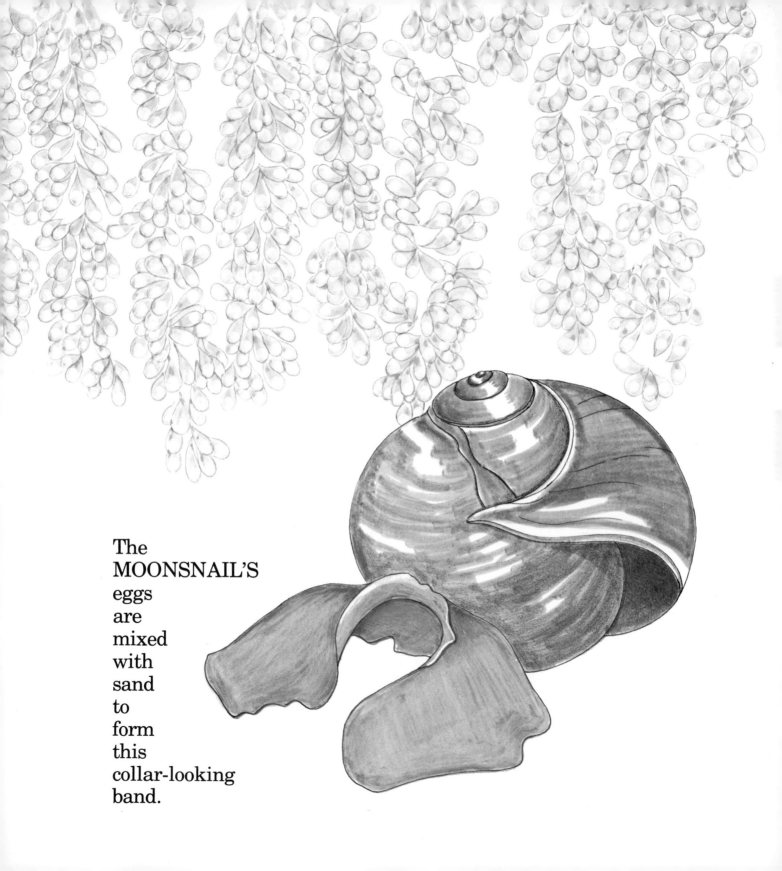

The
MOONSNAIL'S
eggs
are
mixed
with
sand
to
form
this
collar-looking
band.

SPIDERS
wrap
their
eggs
in
sacs;
and

SNAILS,
you
know,
are
very
slow,
but
they
lay
eggs
that
hatch
and
grow,

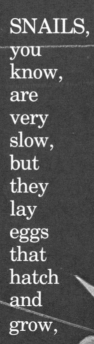

and so do . . .

INSECTS

who
have
six
legs
and
lay
many
different
kinds
of eggs.

This
one

will
hatch
into a
hungry
CATERPIL
who . . .
will

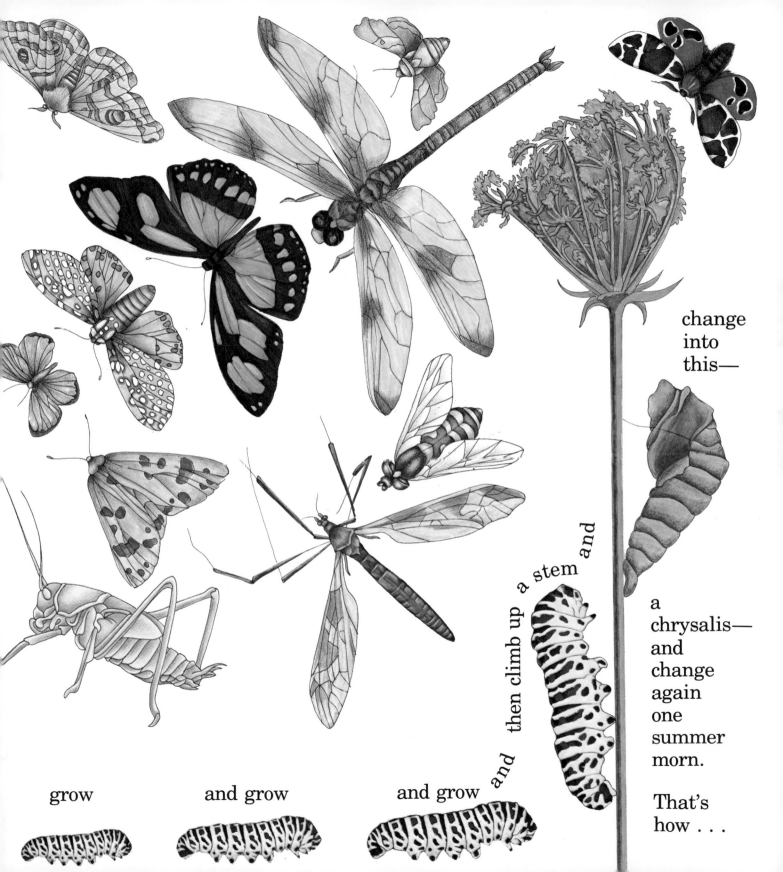

change
into
this—

a
chrysalis—
and
change
again
one
summer
morn.

That's
how . . .

and then climb up a stem and

and

grow   and grow   and grow

a BUTTERFLY is born.

Animals with fur or hair
who nurse their young
and don't lay eggs
are known as MAMMALS or
MAMMALIA.

SPINY ANTEATER

But these are two exceptions,
and they both live in
Australia.

DUCKBILL PLATYPUS

CHICKENS aren't the only ones.
There's no more to discuss.
Everyone who
lays an egg
is
O · VIP · A · ROUS.

Animals
who don't
lay eggs
have babies
born
alive and well,
but
that's
another
tale
to
tell.

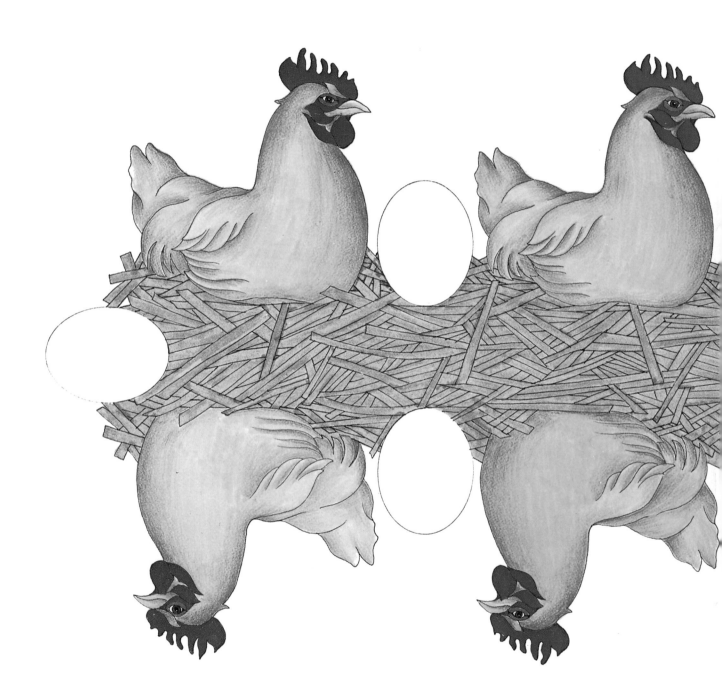

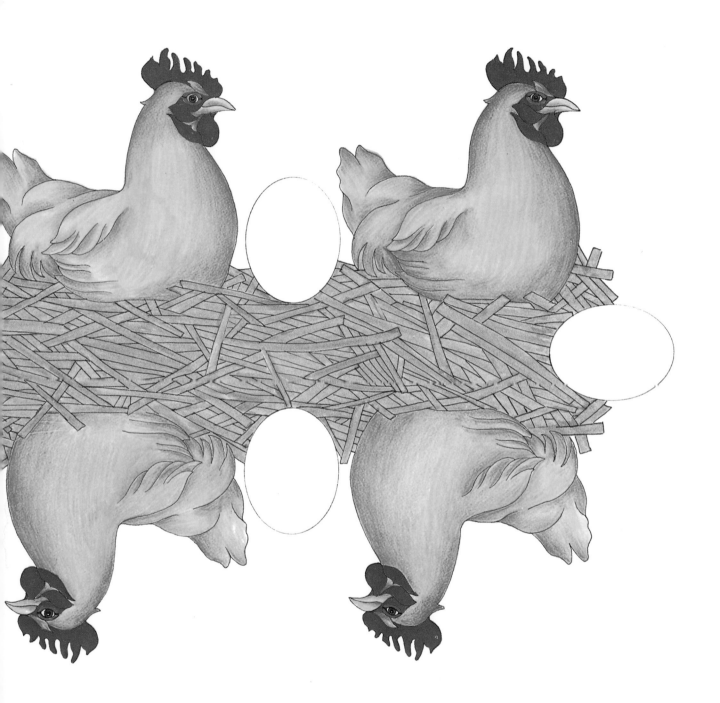